WINNING AT WORK READINESS

STEP-BY-STEP GUIDE TO

WIN-WIN NEGOTIATING EVERY DAY

Alexandra Hanson-Harding

ROSEN
PUBLISHING®

New York

Published in 2015 by The Rosen Publishing Group, Inc.
29 East 21st Street, New York, NY 10010

Copyright © 2015 by The Rosen Publishing Group, Inc.

First Edition

Library of Congress Cataloging-in-Publication Data

Hanson-Harding, Alexandra.
Step-by-step guide to win-win negotiating every day/Alexandra Hanson-Harding.
      pages cm. — (Winning at work readiness)
Includes bibliographical references and index.
Audience: Grade 7 to 12.
ISBN 978-1-4777-7790-9 (library bound) — ISBN 978-1-4777-7792-3 (pbk.)
— ISBN 978-1-4777-7793-0 (6-pack)
1. Negotiation—Juvenile literature. 2. Negotiation in business—Juvenile literature.
I. Title.
BF637.N4H366 2015
302.3'5—dc23

                                                                  2014006342

Manufactured in the United States of America

CONTENTS

INTRODUCTION

Nelson Mandela said, "If you want to make peace with your enemy, you have to work with your enemy. Then he becomes your partner." Antoinette Tuff faced a difficult choice on August 20, 2013. That day, a man carrying an assault rifle and five hundred rounds of ammunition entered the elementary school where she works in the suburbs of Atlanta, Georgia. Should she run? Hide? Beg? Instead, for more than twenty-four minutes, she stayed on the telephone with 911 and negotiated a deal between the mentally ill young man and the police. She told the police to stay away when he ordered her to. Understanding his act as a desperate cry for help, she told him about hard times in her life, too. Finally, she persuaded him to put his gun on a table, lie down with his arms behind his back, and let the police take him away. After it was over, she admitted she'd been terrified. In a CNN interview, Chris Voss, a former FBI hostage negotiator, said Tuff's performance was "amazing." "She didn't do anything where she acted like a victim," Voss said. "She didn't say, 'Please, don't hurt anybody.' She was very direct."

Not everyone will face a hostage situation like Antoinette Tuff did. But if you're like most people, you do some kind of negotiating every day, whether it's over a Saturday night curfew, how to sell raffle tickets for a soccer team fund-raiser, or what to do when your brother wears your favorite shirt. Being able to negotiate can also help you further a cause you believe in.

"All of us negotiate many times a day," says negotiation expert Richard Shell, author of *Bargaining for Advantage*. What exactly is negotiation? Shell describes it as "an interactive process that may take place whenever we want something from someone else or another person wants something from us."

Antoinette Tuff's courage and skill at negotiating saved her school from a disturbed gunman.

This text is about "win-win" negotiating. This type of negotiating involves two parties working through a conflict as partners. Although each person can fight hard for her own side, in the end, both parties are usually at least somewhat satisfied. In this text, you will learn how to use win-win negotiation as a toolbox to resolve conflicts in a way that will bring you—and others— long-term benefits.

Chapter 1

WHAT KINDS OF NEGOTIATION ARE THERE?

The willingness to negotiate can make a tremendous difference in people's lives. For example, according to economics professor Linda Babcock, coauthor of *Women Don't Ask*, men start negotiations approximately four times as often as women. And when women do negotiate, they ask for 30 percent less than men do. Babcock cites studies saying that the failure to negotiate for salary means that women lose out on between $500,000 and $1 million over the course of their careers. Holly Schroth, a social psychologist at the University of California, Berkeley, says, "If you don't ask, you don't get." Babcock has helped start a program at Carnegie Mellon University to assist both women and girls. They can develop negotiation skills that they can use to get better salaries and make other important deals in their life and work.

When people negotiate, they learn to stand up for themselves and for things they value. If they are strong, persuasive, and skillful but fair as negotiators, they are likely to convince the other side that they are intelligent and rational people to work with. In effect, they are advertising their negotiating skills by the *way* they negotiate! The way others perceive them is essential to making sure that

Be wary of writing to someone when angry. The other person can't see the writer's facial expressions, and the words can seem more harsh than when two people are face-to-face.

people are not just willing to make promises but agree to follow through on them. There are four basic negotiating styles anyone can use.

LOSE-WIN

In lose-win negotiation, someone basically gives up before he begins. This is most often used by people who feel weak or who dislike bargaining. The problem with lose-win is that often the person who does it wants to seem "nice" but can come off as weak. Instead of being appreciated for his generosity, he could be seen as someone easy to push around.

Even if someone is angry, it's helpful to keep cool in an argument.

LOSE-LOSE

Lose-lose negotiating occurs when both parties fight so viciously that they both end up worse off at the end of the negotiation than they were at the beginning. They lose any reason to feel loyalty toward each other and may seek revenge. If one friend gets so mad at another friend that she spills his secrets to a third friend, for example, he might share her secrets in return.

HANI KHAN, ALL-AMERICAN GIRL

One powerful reason people negotiate is because they are seeking justice. When Hani Khan was growing up in Foster City, California, she always felt comfortable wearing her hijab, or Muslim head covering. "After 9/11, all my neighbors, all my classmates, all my teachers . . . supported me," Khan told the *South San Francisco Patch*. She even got a job at the clothing store Abercrombie and Fitch. The company has a policy of hiring people who have an "All-American" look, and to promote it they have a strict "Look Policy." Khan's boss said that as long as she wore a hijab in the store's colors, she would meet the dress code. But after a high-ranking manager came to the store, Khan was ordered to not wear her headscarf. She refused. Soon, she was fired. She was shocked by the experience. In a news conference, Khan said the firing "shook my confidence. I didn't have that problem before." She added, "For there to be an issue now, it was just completely out of the ordinary."

She believed Abercrombie and Fitch was wrong to fire her. She tried talking to the company but got nowhere. But she wouldn't give up. She got some extra help—from lawyers—and sued the company. In 2013, she won. Because of the tolerance she had received growing up, her persistence, and her belief in herself, she helped herself win justice and helped Abercrombie and Fitch win by helping it enlarge its understanding of what a real "All-American" look is—one that includes people of different faiths.

WIN-LOSE

Win-lose negotiation is negotiating to win no matter what the cost. When bargaining for a car, for instance, it can make sense to bargain hard because one will probably never see the car salesman again. However, if the deal includes working with another person, the problem with win-lose negotiation is that many times, it also leaves bitterness behind. If you demand too many rides to a friend's house, your mom might say that it's too much trouble and refuse to give you any rides at all.

WIN-WIN

Win-win means negotiating so that two parties agree to address a problem and try to find a solution together. Win-win negotiation is when both sides come out of the negotiation feeling as if they have been treated fairly, even if one party gets more than the other. It is a form of negotiation based on respect.

NECESSARY TECHNIQUES TO NEGOTIATE

Even if a person enters a negotiation with a desire to be civil, she should not go unarmed. She needs to understand the basic rules and techniques of negotiating. Her opponent is in conflict with her. As much as she wants the problem solving to be mutually beneficial, the problem she most wants to solve, the goal she most wants to reach, is her own. That is the bottom line. And that is why it is important to know what that goal is—and to have it written down. She also needs to understand the ground rules of negotiating and learn how to turn them to her advantage.

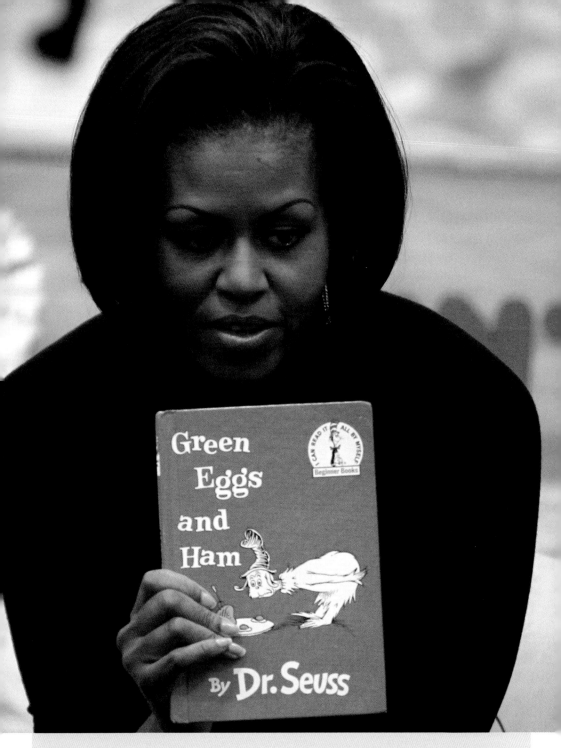

First Lady Michelle Obama holds Dr. Seuss's classic book *Green Eggs and Ham*, a story that models persistence.

An example of a valuable technique is sheer persistence. Remember the Dr. Seuss story *Green Eggs and Ham*? One finicky character refuses to try green eggs and ham again and again, saying, "But I do not like Green Eggs and Ham. I will not eat them, Sam I am." Sam I Am repeated his offer again and again— and, as Stuart Diamond, author of *How You Can Negotiate and Succeed in Work and Life* said, "After more than 100 lovely requests and denials, green eggs and ham are happily eaten." Talk about a win-win situation! If you believe in your goal, stick with it. Sometimes your opponents may just not know how good your offer is.

Chapter 2

CHOOSING YOUR BATTLES

One of the most valuable tools any negotiator can have is knowing what *not* to negotiate. Some conflicts are so small that they aren't worth fighting about. Others are so big that they need the help of adults. Still others can be deflected with a straightforward "no."

TOO SMALL TO FIGHT

When something small is irritating, try to reframe, or get a different perspective on it. Get a reputation for being someone with an open heart and kindness, and you'll have credibility when you most need it.

BE TOLERANT

When he was in high school, some people thought they could upset actor James Franco by calling him gay. But the actor has many gay friends. He just shrugged the comments off. "It wasn't something that frightened me, like if people think that [I'm gay], it's fine. I really don't care," he said in an MTV interview posted

Actor James Franco has played many roles, but he knows who he really is. Because of his confidence, he can't be baited or dragged into unnecessary debates about his identity.

on the *Huffington Post* website. If you're open-minded, then being attacked for being gay, straight, the wrong religion, etc., won't hurt because you accept other people anyway.

GIVE A FREE PASS

If a friend acts cranky at a party, but she's normally OK, perhaps it can just be ignored. But don't let it become a habit.

SAY IT'S PART OF THE PACKAGE

Maybe a friend is dreamy and artistic, but he's less on time than others. One choice is to keep criticizing him for being fifteen minutes late. Alternately, you can remember the qualities you like about him, such as being funny or nice, and just say that this is part of his temperament and that different people are different.

AGREE TO DISAGREE

Your boyfriend's idea of a perfect weekend involves six football games on TV, and you'd rather do long-distance running. Don't be mad! Be independent! Join the track team and enjoy giving each other some time apart. Having separate interests can be healthy, both for friends and people in relationships.

Just because people are in relationships doesn't mean that they can't have separate interests, such as running. Enjoy your differences!

15

RESPECT DIFFERENCES

Some of the most interesting perspectives come from people who may have a different background than your own. Rather than debating, try having open discussions where you try to be genuinely interested in people's different religions and cultures. Instead of trying to persuade other people to join your political party or religion, try to find common ground.

AVOID TEMPTATION

Sometimes it might be tempting to argue for something that doesn't deserve it—like asking a parent to buy an expensive pair of boots you don't really need. It's hard not to feel bombarded by constant media images that tell us how to dress and what to eat and buy. So before you ask, imagine what would be considered fair by an objective third party. Be as fair and mature as you can.

TOO BIG

Sometimes young people face dangerous or questionable situations that require adult help. In those cases, getting adult help is the most mature thing to do.

SPEAK UP!

In West Albany, Oregon, seventeen-year-old Truman Templeton heard a fellow student bragging about how he could make bombs. Truman didn't know whether the boy was joking or not, but the other student's behavior was strange. Truman nervously decided to report it. When police examined the other student's house, they found that the student had six homemade bombs in his bedroom and a timeline of how he was going to kill people. "I'd much rather report something like this than leave it alone," Truman said. "All I can say is what story would you want to see on the news? One person being arrested or dozens of kids dying because of a disaster that could have been prevented?" he asked ABC News affiliate KATU-TV.

DANGEROUS RELATIONSHIPS

If a boyfriend is overly controlling—if he checks on you with constant texts, tries to separate you from friends or family, or threatens to harm himself or you, get out of that situation immediately. Because controlling people can be dangerous when people turn against them, get the help of a smart grown-up about how to safely end a controlling relationship.

THE CODE OF SECRECY

Sometimes friends beg you to keep secrets about their harmful habits. If a friend is doing something to hurt herself, she may be using those actions as a cry for help. Even if she lashes out at you for telling a responsible adult that she is doing things such as cutting, threatening suicide, or abusing drugs, she may thank you later.

ITEMS YOU *WON'T* NEGOTIATE

Sometimes the world of parents can seem very different than the world of today's youth. In many schools, a significant number of students have either tried or at least have access to different kinds of drugs or alcohol. Students are pressured to either participate in trying illegal substances or ignore when other students are

It's helpful to think of ways to say "no" to things that you don't want to do, such as getting involved with drugs.

using them. This can create some uncomfortable dilemmas. Friends may pressure you to "just try" drinking or drugs—or not to tell on them. In that kind of situation, it's important to understand one's own personal boundaries and be able to decide where to draw the line.

What are boundaries? Boundaries are like an electric fence that protects your deepest self, including your passions, your rights, and especially your values. If someone gets too close to your "fence," you automatically feel a warning buzz that something is not right and act on it. Developing boundaries lets you be free and safe. It lets you know what you stand for and who you truly are.

THE POWER OF NO

One way to develop boundaries is by learning to say "no" to things you don't agree with. Some authors have even suggested that until you can say "no," you can't truly say "yes." In an article in *Psychology Today*, Judith Sills suggests that learning to say a simple "no" to things that cross your boundary can be powerful and healthy. If someone offers you beer, you can just say, "No, thank you." You don't owe any explanation.

"I used to say 'yes' to everything because I didn't want to disappoint people in my life, or I wanted people to like me. Then, I would complain about it," says Dr. Christina Hibbert. "I have learned that saying 'no' to someone else is really saying 'yes' to something that's more important to me. It's easier to do this when I'm clear on what really matters to me."

Living by your own boundaries can help other people, too. If there is a cause you believe in—saving animals, feeding the hungry, working for a political cause—knowing who you are and what your values are could give you an extra push to join a group to help. If you see someone being bullied, living by your boundaries

Actor Wentworth Miller made a stand for his values by not going to Russia in protest of its antigay policies.

and personal values could convince you to stand up for the victim instead of just being a bystander. In many situations, all it takes is one person to stand up and object in order to stop the bullying in its tracks.

Wentworth Miller, an actor in the television show *Prison Break*, explained to Lydia Smith that he had a "no" moment when he was invited to attend a film festival in Russia. Russia has a strong antigay policy. He made a public statement that he was gay and would not go anywhere that oppressed gay people. It was the first time he had publically come out as gay. Was it win-win? Yes, because it invited Russia to become a more just society. And because it encouraged other young people to stay strong and have hope for their futures. And Miller no longer had to keep his true self a secret. Many of his fellow actors applauded his courage in taking a stand.

Chapter 3

PREPARING YOUR CASE

If a problem can't be reframed, it may be time to enter into a more serious negotiation. If so, there is no substitute for preparation. Get a journal and start writing down your main concerns and what some possible solutions might be. Circle your most desired goal. As author Stuart Diamond says, "Studies show that goal setting is one of the most important things someone can do for themselves. The mere act of setting a goal has been shown to increase performance by 25 percent." He adds, "There is no point in negotiating at all if you don't have a goal that you want to achieve."

Singer Carrie Rae Jepson has a fun way of figuring out how to figure out her goals. She told *Seventeen* magazine, "I'd pin old bedsheets to the wall and take colorful markers and write where I wanted to be and what I needed to

Keeping a journal is a good way to keep track of goals, and it offers a release for uncomfortable feelings.

Singer Carrie Rae Jepson had a big hit with her single "Call Me Maybe." She has fun ways to set her goals.

do to get there. . . . It's how I have made every great decision in my life." Not everyone needs a whole bedsheet, but many will probably need at least a piece of paper and a pen.

INTERESTS AND POSITIONS

As you figure out your goal, try to think about both your positions and interests. These are described by William Ury, Roger Fisher, and Bruce Patton in their book *Getting to Yes*. For example, if twin sisters are arguing about how to spend their birthday, they could argue forever about whether to have it at a Mexican restaurant or a bowling alley. Those would be positions. But their interests are that they really both want to have a fun birthday and be together. If they focus on that goal, they might come up with some way either to combine their desires or come up with some entirely new solution—like a roller-skating party. In other words, positions are the hard, factual items that people argue about on the surface, such as the price someone wants to pay for a hat, a specific movie she wants to see, or a certain summer camp he wants to attend. Interests are about the underlying needs of the parties—such as respect, social connection, and the opportunity to learn and grow. Often, the deepest need people have is not an item. It is the feeling of being heard. Ury, Fisher, and Patton urge people to use interest-based negotiation over position-based negotiation whenever possible.

UNDERSTAND WHAT THE PARTIES REALLY WANT

Before entering a negotiation, think about what you want and why you want it. There's a classic story about negotiating. Two chefs are arguing about an orange—the only orange they have.

If two chefs disagree about how to use an ingredient, it could make sense for them to discuss what they want to use it for.

They battle fiercely for the precious piece of fruit. That is, until they realize that one chef wants the orange's skin so that he can use its peel for a special frosting. The other cook wants the orange itself because he wants to squeeze its juice into a recipe for cake. They could share the same orange. It could be that you, too, could make a deal where you and your opponent could actually share something because you have different goals for it. Or you could give something of little value as a trade. Maybe a bike that's just sitting in your garage because you no longer ride it would make a perfect trade for a drum set that a friend's parents won't let him keep.

WORKSHEET FOR CLARIFYING GOALS

Before negotiating, answer these questions. On a separate piece of paper, write the following:

1. What is my *position* (main problem or goal)?

2. What is my *interest* (why do I have this goal)? For example:
   a. Does it increase fairness?
   b. Does it develop my dreams?
   c. Does it help me save or get more resources?

3. How do I want the other party to help me reach my goal?

4. What am I prepared to trade?

5. What reasons, including evidence, claims, examples, appeals to fairness, etc., do I have that would persuade the other party to help me?

6. How will it benefit the other party to help me?

7. Have I done anything to reach my goal?

8. What is my BATNA?

PREPARE YOURSELF SO YOU WON'T ACCEPT A BAD DEAL

In the heat of negotiating, people can imagine the other side's offer is more valuable than it actually is and pay too high a price to get it. This can be called winner's remorse. The Harvard Law School Program on Negotiation offers the following example: A professor puts a jar full of coins on his desk and announces he's auctioning it off. The winner could keep it for that price. The winner paid $45 for the coins. As soon as the auction was over, the professor asked how the student felt. The young man was unhappy. He had winner's remorse. He was right. The coins were worth only $20. Always ask: Is this meeting my goals? Don't forget your interests and your BATNA. What's a BATNA? That's the walking away point in a deal.

BRING ON YOUR BATNA!

The authors of *Getting to Yes* developed the term "BATNA," or "Best Alternative to a Negotiated Agreement." That means, basically, the best outcome you could have if you walked away from the deal the other party offered you. Fisher, Ury, and Patton wrote that the three best ways to develop a BATNA are as follows:

1. Write down a list of alternatives.
2. Turn the best ones into practical options.
3. Choose the best if no deal is reached.

What is the best possible outcome that you would have if you walk away from this deal? Say you are selling an old longboard after switching to a new style of skateboard. You advertise it for $75, and some guy offers $30. Some factors to consider are how

When someone has something to sell, such as a longboard, he chooses how much he values it when he sets a price on it.

desperate you are for cash and how likely it is for someone else to make a better offer. If you're not willing to sell for less than $60, not in a rush for money, and know that longboards are a popular item, your BATNA might be to let the longboard stay in the basement until someone offers you more for it. By telling the other party that you know it's worth more than $30 and you aren't in a hurry to sell, that strong BATNA might persuade the other party to raise his offer.

Stuart Diamond says, "Goals are the be-all and end-all of negotiations. You negotiate to meet your goals. Everything else is subservient to that." He adds, "Goals are what you are trying to accomplish. Don't try to establish a relationship unless it brings you closer to your goals. Don't deal with others' interests or needs or feelings or anything else unless it brings you closer to your goals. Don't give or get information unless it brings you closer to your goals."

Chapter 4

GETTING THE OTHER PARTY TO THE TABLE

What leverage (power) do you have to get your opponent to meet with you? One way to figure that out is to take another piece of paper and answer the same questions you answered for yourself in chapter 3—but this time, imagine her point of view. What does she *really* want?

Research this opponent by observing her or by asking other people. Is she reasonable? Does your opponent have certain "hot buttons" that will irritate her? Does she have anything she particularly values that you can offer? As you write the list, you may find points of agreement. Circle them. They may be a starting place to build goodwill into your negotiation.

THE STICK, THE CARROT, AND THE HUG

To get someone to negotiate, three different kinds of power can be used, according to peace researcher and economist Kenneth Boulding: the stick, the carrot, and the hug.

When two partners figure out what roles they will take on a school project, they might try to find areas of agreement before they negotiate their roles.

THE STICK

Sometimes you need to get tough to get the other party to negotiate. That's when it's time for the stick. One method is by refusing to cooperate with the other party until he or she negotiates. Another motivation is, especially for businesses, protection of reputation. If, for example, a store won't let you return a sweater that had a hole in it when it was purchased, you can threaten to write a letter of complaint. The bottom line of using the stick is enforcing consequences for what one sees as genuinely unfair,

31

This illustration of a classic Aesop's fable shows that sometimes being too hard and cold (like the harsh wind) can make people resist opening up.

unprofessional, or immoral behavior. If you don't get good results, you can even bring it to a third party. For example, if a classmate is doing nothing on a group project, you can warn her that you are going to ask the teacher for a new partner if she doesn't cooperate.

THE CARROT

A carrot approach is one where the parties have something to trade. For example, in his book *Outliers*, author Malcolm Gladwell tells the story of how, when Microsoft CEO Bill Gates was growing up, his junior high school was one of the few in the country that had a computer club. But buying computer time was expensive. Finally, one company was willing to trade computer time to the kids if they promised to spend their weekends debugging (fixing) the company's new software programs. Gates and his friends were hooked. The trade was a total win-win negotiation. This carrot helped the company and gave young Bill Gates experience that put him miles ahead of his peers.

THE HUG

The old expression, "Honey catches flies faster than vinegar," or the following Aesop's fable explain the hug approach. The sun and the north wind had a contest to see who could do a better job of making a man remove his heavy cloak. First, the wind blew and blew—but instead of blowing the cloak off, the man pulled it tight around him. Then the hot sun came out, and in its warmth, the man no longer needed to protect himself, so he took the cloak off. That is the spirit behind the "hug" approach. It could be an appeal to fairness—asking the other person to negotiate to address some kind of injustice. Another way is asking for help to improve your relationship with the person. If you need to work or live with someone, she is already invested in your satisfaction because if you are unhappy, you may be less cooperative in ways that affect her life. As Kenneth Boulding said in his book *Three Faces of Power*, "The stick, the carrot, and the hug may all be necessary but the greatest of these is the hug."

POISONING THE WELL AND OTHER FALLACIES

Before engaging in a debate, be aware that some people may not fight fairly. They may try to introduce unfair or misleading claims, called fallacies, to influence a deal. One of these is called "poisoning the well" and was first used by John Henry Newman in 1864. He used it do describe a situation when someone smears another's reputation so that he or she won't seem credible when later bringing up a point in an argument. If people use this, try to respond calmly by asking the other party to stick to the topic. If the person doesn't, call a time-out until he or she does. Here are just a few logical fallacies:

Ad hominem attacks: Attacking the person, not the problem—for example, saying that nobody would trust a klutz like you to know anything about ice-skating. Your coordination and your knowledge are two different things. These kinds of attacks can be nasty and personal, so call out any opponent who uses them.

Diversion: Attacking by diversion. If you are discussing curfews and your opponent suggests that you wouldn't need to stay out late if you weren't such a slob, this is a fallacy because neatness has nothing to do with staying out late. It's simply meant to take attention away from the real issue at hand.

Red herrings: Bringing up an issue that is not relevant to the issue. For example, if you go to a flea market and offer $5 for a hat, and the seller insists she could only take $10 because it came from Japan, the fact that the hat came from Japan is a red herring because where the hat came from doesn't matter.

Slippery slope: A series of illogical jumps in a claim. If you ask to keep a kitten you found in your yard, and a parent makes some kind of exaggerating statement about how if you have one kitten, pretty soon you'll have thirty, that's a slippery slope. Plenty of people manage to hold the line at one cat.

SETTING THE STRATEGY

Once an opponent has agreed to meet with you, it's a good idea to consider the best underlying strategy to use to conduct the negotiation. You may both agree to fight as hard as you can for your sides (i.e., win-lose negotiating). A gentler approach could be what Behance Corporation CEO Scott Belsky says in an article on OpenForum.com: "When negotiating a deal that will yield a relationship, you'll want to consider the 'fairness' strategy. It's simple: Have a discussion up front with your counterpart in the negotiation. Make the case that, philosophically, you want to reach the fairest deal for both parties. Then, in preparing to make your offer, put yourself in your counterpart's shoes to determine what they should fairly expect (and deserve). Do the same thing for yourself."

Chapter 5

NEGOTIATING

S ometimes an issue needs to be negotiated more formally to settle more complicated issues. Once all preparations have been made, and both sides have agreed to meet, there are several steps to take.

AGREE ON A TIME AND PLACE

There's no point trying to negotiate with someone who is distracted, on her way out the door, or in a bad mood. Try to pick a time that works for both parties. Sometimes it helps to go into a private place, like an empty classroom, or to another kind of neutral place, such as a local café or a park. When you sit together, make sure that the seating is fair—don't have one person sit with the sun in her eyes and the other sit in comfort on the other side of the table.

USE STRONG BODY LANGUAGE

Be relaxed and confident. A rigid posture can send the message that you are nervous or defensive, but also don't fidget. Don't let

This young man's good posture and confident expression make it clear that he's ready to talk business.

people tower over you or physically intimidate you. Don't be arrogant, but be an equal.

CRAFT AN OPENING STATEMENT

Either party can make the first statement. It's often good if you can keep silent and let the other party start because that gives you information that you might not have had before. But there are also advantages to starting first. Whoever makes the first offer can "anchor" the discussion, or, in other words, set the terms of the discussion. One good strategy for the person who makes the first statement is to open up the negotiations by saying how important this relationship is. (As many negotiators say, the relationship between people can make or break a deal.) Then he should state his goal, why he deserves to get it, and why it's good for the other party, too. And, says negotiator Roger Dawson, author of *The Secrets of Power Negotiating*, be sure to have the courage to ask for more than you expect to get. That's because it's easier to back down from your initial demand than it is to ask for more later.

DON'T TAKE THE FIRST OFFER

Never accept the other party's first proposal, says Dawson—in fact, he suggests flinching when the person suggests it, as if it's too shocking to be real. Dawson says to flinch because most people think visually; if they see a sign of disappointment, they will react. By accepting the first offer that the other party makes, you could actually end up disappointing your opponent and making him sorry he didn't ask for more.

By looking shocked or disappointed at the first offer you receive in a negotiation, you may end up receiving a better one.

PRACTICE ACTIVE LISTENING

Active listening isn't just letting people ramble on until they run out of things to say. It's a structured way of listening and responding. If someone says that he feels it's not fair that he has to do all the work on a project, a good response might be to use an I-statement that reflects that you sense his frustration when it seems as if other people aren't doing their share. Reflecting back statements in this way allows the speaker to know if his words have been understood. He can correct the record if they aren't. Listen not just for what the opponent says, but how he says it.

Dawson says that *who*, *where*, *what*, *why*, and *how* questions work better than questions the other party can answer with yes or no. Examples include the following:

- What is your biggest concern?
- How can we both be satisfied?
- Where would you rather go?

BE AWARE OF NONVERBAL CLUES

If people are upset, they can show their feelings without saying a word. Some examples of resistant or defensive behavior include leaning back in their chairs, crossing their arms or legs, interrupting to take a texting break, looking away, frowning, standing up, or shaking their heads. When an opponent looks backed into a corner, he is probably not listening to what is being said. That might be a clue to either stop talking or to ask an open-ended question to start the conversation again.

What can you guess about the attitude of the men in this picture from their body language?

KEEP IT COOL

If you find yourself getting emotional, one way to keep cool is by using a special kind of breathing technique called controlled breathing. According to an article in *Time* magazine titled "6 Breathing Exercises to Relax in 10 Minutes or Less," controlled breathing can help a negotiator calm and lower stress. In the article, yoga instructor Rebecca Pacheco recommends a technique called equal breathing. That is, count to four as you inhale through the nose. Then exhale to the count of four, also through your nose. Pacheco says using the nose adds a natural resistance to the breath and should help reduce stress and increase focus. If that doesn't work, call for a time-out immediately and regroup. Don't be ashamed, don't look back, but just proceed from that moment.

If the other party is losing his temper and screaming or talking over you, call him out on his bad behavior immediately. Telling opponents that you can't take in what they're saying if they're screaming, or telling them that you feel uncomfortable when you're being interrupted constantly, will give them the message that they can't manipulate you by using bad behavior. If someone is really in a rage, tell him you'll talk to him later. When people are talking about issues important to them, they can get emotional. Don't allow them to bully, but don't take their anger personally, either. Remember your goal.

TECHNIQUES THAT ACTUALLY PERSUADE PEOPLE

The simplest technique is the most obvious: be seen as trustworthy and credible. Show good faith and put people at ease. But also be charming and tough.

APPEALING TO FAIRNESS

If a new family in town hires you as a babysitter and pays $8 an hour when other sitters get $10, you could argue for more by appealing to fairness. You could tell the father that the standard rate in town is $10 an hour. He might argue that you hadn't agreed on a rate beforehand. You might argue back that if he tried to get another babysitter for less, he might be out of luck—and that you pride yourself on doing a good job with kids. You might suggest that he would naturally want the best care he could get for his child and that this was not a good area to skimp. It could be hard to argue against those arguments. Most parents would not like to think that they would get bad care for their children, and they also would not like to be stuck without babysitters.

FINDING POINTS OF AGREEMENT AND DISAGREEMENT

Knowing what you *don't* have to argue about helps to focus the argument. If the planning committee for the varsity soccer dinner has to choose between prune surprise and chocolate cake, it makes negotiation easier if the committee can agree on the latter. Sometimes knowing what everyone disagrees on can be helpful, too—any issue that everyone can "agree to disagree on" can be taken off the table. You can tell your friend that you know she loves gory movies, but since they give you nightmares, maybe there's some other kind of activity you can have at the sleepover.

BEING PERSISTENT

Return to the main point. Don't get sidetracked. Be persistent. Say you want a dog. Try to find ways that having a dog would be beneficial not just to you, but to the whole family. For example, you might find an article about the value of watchdogs or about the health benefits of walking a dog. Look for statistics and anecdotes about the benefits of having a dog. Another way of being persuasive is appealing to your parents' or guardians' sense of pity.

Being willing to walk a neighbor's dogs is one way to demonstrate a commitment to your goal.

You can tell them about how many perfectly healthy dogs are killed at shelters because no one will take them home. An even more persuasive technique is demonstrating how you would be a responsible dog owner. You could walk a neighbor dog and clean up after it. Or even be more helpful at home. This might convince your parents that you wouldn't leave the burden of cleaning up after a pet with them. The more rational and mature you sound, the better. But keep returning to it if it really matters to you. When should you give up? It's up to you. It's over when *you* say it's over.

GIRL GONE VIRAL

More than two million YouTube watchers have viewed Rachel Parent, age fourteen, debate Canadian TV show host Kevin O'Leary. They saw a young person use persistence, dignity, and courage to get across her views—and even to get the host to agree with her, almost in spite of himself. The Ontario teen started researching GMOs (genetically modified organisms) in junior high. GMOs are plants and animals created through gene splicing. She found what she learned troubling, so she started a group called Kids Right to Know, which urges the government to label GMO foods. When she got the chance to speak on the famous Canadian TV show *Lang and O'Leary*, she jumped at the chance.

Rachel did three of the smartest things any negotiator can do: She kept her cool, she knew her subject, and she stayed on message. She even got O'Leary to agree with her major points—that GMOs should be labeled so that people who don't want to buy them can identify them. Whether or not you agree with her point, you can learn from her calmness under pressure. Was it a win-win? It brought publicity to O'Leary's show and to Rachel's cause. Here is part of it:

Host Kevin O'Leary: Do you think you are a lobbyist for the movement that's against genetically modified foods?
Rachel Parent: No. I don't think so. I think that I'm just a part of that movement.
O'Leary: Do you make the assumption . . . that all kids of your age believe that this is a bad thing to experiment with foods?

Parent: Not necessarily. But I believe that everyone has the right to know what's in their food. . . . I just want GMO labeling and that way people can make informed decisions.
O'Leary: [My daughter] said, "I am going to examine both sides." And I wish for you the same thing.
Parent: Actually, I have examined both sides, but I choose to follow this side.
O'Leary: OK, different issue around labeling. I think everybody gets that and I think the trend in society now is more transparency, and you are going to get labeling.

USE TIME WISELY

Many negotiations don't flow. They have stops and starts. Both participants may want to slow down or speed up negotiations depending on whether or not it benefits them. Use time to prolong or shorten the negotiation until you're satisfied. Sometimes a cooling-off period is needed to let the parties weigh their options.

Conversely, one party may have more time pressure than the other. The day before the junior prom, maybe you discovered your date actually *did* expect to get a corsage. Even though you thought the flowered wristband was ridiculously expensive, you were not in a good position to bargain with the florist at that late date. But if you went to a yard sale on a Sunday afternoon and found a tempting piece of sports equipment, the owner might be willing to bargain just to get you to take it away.

Another way you can use time, even if your opponents don't agree with your goal, is to ask them to think about it. Ask if they would mind keeping your idea in their head for the next week? Sometimes giving people time to think makes them change their minds.

Chapter 6

FROM STUCK TO DONE

Negotiators sometimes refer to the object of the negotiation as "the pie." If one party thinks that the other side is trying to get all the "slices" of the pie, he or she can get angry. Negotiations can get deadlocked this way.

"Enlarging the pie" is adding new ideas, items, or services that might make a deal more attractive. An example of enlarging the pie could include offering your parents one weekend night of babysitting a month if they agree to pay for your saxophone lessons. That means they won't have to pay for a babysitter (so more money to pay for those lessons), and you can just chill at home one weekend night with your siblings.

MAKING CONCESSIONS

In negotiating, it makes the other party feel more successful and in control if he feels he has gotten something concrete out of the deal. So look for opportunities to give the other person something in return. In Mark Twain's novel *Tom Sawyer*, Tom was being punished by having to whitewash a fence. But Tom got an idea. He

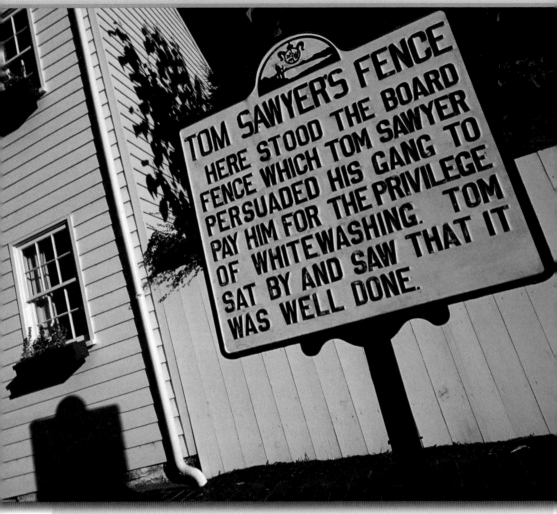

TOM SAWYER'S FENCE
HERE STOOD THE BOARD
FENCE WHICH TOM SAWYER
PERSUADED HIS GANG TO
PAY HIM FOR THE PRIVILEGE
OF WHITEWASHING. TOM
SAT BY AND SAW THAT IT
WAS WELL DONE.

Making a job seem fun the way Tom Sawyer did in Mark Twain's classic story is an effective negotiating tool.

started whitewashing (or painting) with a happy look on his face. Soon, another boy stopped by and was intrigued by how much fun Tom was having. Tom let him try whitewashing, too—for a small price. Tom put up a sign advertising the opportunity to white-wash, and other boys started lining up. Even if it was a bit of a trick, both parties won: Tom made money off his punishment, but the other boys had a good time, too.

HAGGLING

When someone truly gets into a negotiation, she will probably find herself entering the haggling stage. This is the time to play hardball—with a smile. This can be hard for anyone, but especially girls. One of the findings of Rachel Simmons, cofounder of the Girls Leadership Institute, is: "Girls and women intuit that speaking up can be dangerous to your reputation—that asking for too much can be viewed as conceited or cocky." This is where preparation counts. If someone is negotiating for a raise, the secret is not letting the negotiating get personal. She should view it as something outside of her boundaries. It's not being arrogant if one is just making reasonable points.

Say you want to move to the guest room because you think your brother is a slob. Before negotiating, make a list of points that are as fair and reasonable as possible. Imagine what your opponent's objections would be. For example, what would happen if a guest came? You could offer to stay with your brother for that time. The more reasonable questions you can answer, and the better the case you make, the more confidence you will get. If you get an unexpected question, you can always ask what your parents think would be a good solution.

Consider another approach if you wanted to leave home and move in with some friends after high school. You might present the idea to your father. Maybe your dad rejects it. The next day, instead of pushing your opinion harder, perhaps tell your father about your worries about the idea of moving. You could say you are concerned about living with roommates, cooking, how you will be able to handle money, and so on. You might find that by voicing your fears, your father would know that you understand the risks of moving out. He might start arguing on the other side—that it could help you develop responsibility, that you are competent, and that he could give you some helpful tips. That way, you might not

Learning how to come to a final agreement is a skill that can be learned with practice.

only get your dad's full support, but you might learn useful things from him as well.

Negotiating can be scary at first. It takes nerve to stand up to others, be willing to reject poor offers, and get down to the nitty-gritty. But after doing it a few times, negotiation can start to be fun. As Simmons says, "This is about muscles that need to be developed. This is about practice."

COMING TO THE FINAL DEAL

How do people reach the final deal? One way is to ask a question that narrows it down again. One party might ask her opponent which of the ideas that were discussed he thought was the most important to him. Or if you wanted to have a later curfew, you might ask your parents what you could do to convince them you're trustworthy. This is a good time to check your own emotions and those of your opponents.

Even though it may seem as if a deal is in sight, no one should just settle because it's easier, especially if it isn't something he wants to live with long term. No one gets a good reputation if he makes a deal and then doesn't live up to it because he doesn't like it. In the same way, if an opponent is squirming or frowning, find out what emotion is driving her unhappiness. She should feel that she got something worthwhile out of the deal—especially if what she gets doesn't mean that much to her. In fact, sometimes it can help to act dissatisfied or as if an issue of little importance is a big deal. This can put the opponent off guard, so she realizes that you can walk away from the deal, too. That could make her more eager to please.

In any case, once it seems like the issues have been worked out, one way to affirm that both sides understand what they're agreeing to is to have both parties vocalize what they think they're agreeing to. Some expert negotiators believe that once people have spoken the deal they agreed to, they take it more seriously.

WRITE IT OUT TOGETHER AND SIGN IT

Once two parties have reached an agreement, it's helpful to write it down. It doesn't have to be fancy. Just put the date on the top of a piece of paper and write "Mom and Dad agree to _____" on one line and "I agree to _____" on another. On a third line, you can write, "If these conditions are not met, the consequence will be _____." Then both parties can sign the agreement.

What are the signs that a negotiation has been successful? It might come as a surprise to learn that it isn't necessary for both

Sometimes people are happy with a deal, even if they don't get exactly what they want, if they feel understood and respected.

parties to come out with an exactly equal deal. However, both parties should feel like the agreement meets their essential needs. They need to feel respected and listened to. Especially if it involves a long-term commitment, it needs to be fair enough so that each person feels committed to perform his or her part.

Learning the skill of negotiating really can make a difference. It builds confidence, provides training for adult life, and provides the ability to make a difference. As Rachel Parent says, "Whenever anyone tells you [that] you are too young to change the world, they are wrong. We are all connected and it's amazing like how one spark of inspiration can breathe fire into whatever you do and can even change the destiny of an entire nation!"

GLOSSARY

active listening A way of listening that involves asking open-ended questions, listening carefully to the answers, and reflecting back what the speaker said.

anchor A first offer, such as a price, that sets the stage for what at least one of the two parties expects to receives.

BATNA Best Alternative to a Negotiated Agreement; that is, the point at which you're willing to walk away from a deal.

boundaries An internal set of rules or guidelines that protect you from violating your values and sense of self.

conflict Problems or disagreements between two or more parties.

credibility The reputation of a person; how much he or she is trusted.

enlarging the pie Bringing in new ideas, options, and items to trade into a negotiation.

fallacy An error in thinking.

goal What each party wants.

interests The underlying desires that people bring to negotiations.

leverage The power one has over other people.

negotiating A process where two (or more) parties try to work through their conflicts in order to resolve them.

parties The people who are involved in a negotiation.

perceive How one see things.

persuade Getting another person to change his or her behavior or ideas.

position The stated goal of a negotiation.

reframe To take a different perspective.

strategy A plan for accomplishing a large overall goal.

tolerant Open-minded.

trade An exchange of services, goods, or ideas, sometimes as part of a deal or bargain.

unequal trades Trading something that means little to you but much to your opponent, or vice versa.

win When people get more of their goal than they expected.

winner's remorse The feeling of regret a person gets when believing that he or she should have negotiated a better deal than he or she did.

win-win negotiating A style of negotiation that involves both parties working as partners trying to solve a conflict together.

FOR MORE INFORMATION

Canadian International Institute of Applied Negotiation
97 Toms Road
Dacre, ON K0J 1N0
Canada
(613) 237-9050
Website: http://www.ciian.org
This Canadian organization works in many countries to resolve
    conflicts, with special programs for identifying the potential
    for violence before it happens. The website features a news-
    letter, downloadable publications, and more.

Conflict Information Consortium
580 UCB, University of Colorado
Boulder, CO 80309
(303) 492-1635
Website: http://www.beyondintractability.org
This website contains an extensive online encyclopedia of negotia-
    tion terms, essays and overviews, and online audio
    interviews, among other resources for those interested in
    negotiation.

Department of Justice, Government of Canada
284 Wellington Street
Ottawa, ON K1A 0H8
Canada
Website: http://www.justice.gc.ca
Canada's Department of Justice website contains much informa-
    tion about legal matters, including family and youth issues,
    as well as a large Dispute Prevention and Resolution Services
    section, which lays out the process of various forms of nego-
    tiation. The website also contains a number of helpful links.

Program on Negotiation (PON)
Harvard University Law School
Pound Hall, 5th Floor
1563 Massachusetts Avenue
Cambridge, MA 02138
Website: http://www.pon.harvard.edu
The website for Harvard's Program on Negotiation is "dedicated
to developing the theory and practice of negotiation and
dispute resolution." It contains extensive information about
negotiation, from definitions to styles, with free teaching
and student materials, free reports, and a daily blog.

Youth Service America
1101 15th Street NW, Suite 200
Washington, DC 20005
(202) 296 – 2992
Website: http://www.ysa.org
Youth Service America is an organization dedicated to getting
young people involved in projects. This kind of involvement
can be greatly helpful in developing negotiating skills.

WEBSITES

Due to the changing nature of Internet links, Rosen Publishing
has developed an online list of websites related to the subject of
this book. This site is updated regularly. Please use this link to
access the list:

http://www.rosenlinks.com/WAWR/Negot

FOR FURTHER READING

Covey, Sean. *The Six Most Important Decisions You'll Ever Make Personal Workbook*. New York, NY: Simon & Schuster, 2009.

Doeden, Matt. *Conflict Resolution Smarts: How to Communicate, Negotiate, Compromise, and More*. Minneapolis, MN: Lerner Publishing Group, 2012.

Fonseca, Christine. *The Girl Guide: Finding Your Place in a Mixed Up World*. Waco, TX: Prufrock Press, 2013.

Galbraith, Judy, and Jim Delisle. *The Gifted Teen Survival Guide, Smart, Sharp, and Ready for Almost Anything*. Minneapolis, MN: Free Spirit Publishing, 2012.

Hanson-Harding, Alexandra. *Activism: Taking on Women's Issues*. New York, NY: Rosen Publishing, 2013.

Hanson-Harding, Alexandra. *How to Beat Physical Bullying*. New York, NY: Rosen Publishing, 2013.

Karres, Erika V. Shearin. *Mean Chicks, Cliques, and Dirty Tricks*. Avon, MA: Adams Media, 2010.

Leman, Talia. *A Random Book About the Power of Anyone*. New York, NY: Simon & Schuster, 2012.

Lewis, Barbara A. *The Teen Guide to Global Action: How to Connect with Others (Near & Far) to Create Social Change*. Minneapolis, MN: Free Spirit Publishing, 2008.

Lublin, Nancy, with Vanessa Martin and Julia Steers. *Do Something: A Handbook for Young Activists*. New York, NY: Workman Publishing, 2010.

McCollum, Sean. *Managing Conflict Resolution*. New York, NY: Chelsea House, 2009.

Savage, Dan, and Terry Miller. *It Gets Better: Coming Out, Overcoming Bullying, and Creating a Life Worth Living*. New York, NY: Penguin, 2012.

Sommers, Michael A. *Great Interpersonal Skills*. New York, NY: Rosen Publishing, 2008.

BIBLIOGRAPHY

Babcock, Linda, and Sara Laschever. "Interesting Statistics." Women Don't Ask: Negotiations and the Gender Divide. Retrieved November 2, 2013 (http://www. http://www .womendontask.com/stats.html).

Behary, Wendy T. *Disarming the Narcissist: Surviving and Thriving with the Self-Absorbed*. 2nd ed. Oakland, CA: New Harbinger Publications, 2013.

Belsky, Scott. "A New Approach to Negotiating: The Fairness Strategy." OpenForum.com. Retrieved October 31, 2013 (https://www.openforum.com/articles/a-new-approach-to-negotiating-the-fairness-strategy-1).

Bogart, Lee. *Over the Edge: How the Pursuit of Youth by Marketers and the Media Has Changed American Culture*. Chicago, IL: Ivan R. Dee, 2005.

Booth, Jessica. "10 Tips on How to Be a Diva and Get What You Want." Gurl.com, April 10, 2013. Retrieved October 30, 2013 (http://www.gurl.com/2013/04/10/how-to-get-what-you-want-be-a-diva/#1).

Boothman, Nicholas. *Convince Them in 90 Seconds or Less: Make Instant Connections That Pay Off in Business and Life*. New York, NY: Workman Publishing. 2010.

Boulding, Kenneth. *Three Faces of Power*. Newbury Park, CA: Sage, 1989.

Coloroso, Barbara. *The Bully, the Bullied, and the Bystander*. Updated ed. New York, NY: William Morrow Paperbacks. 2009.

Covey, Stephen R. *The Wisdom and Teachings of Stephen R. Covey*. New York, NY: Free Press, 2012.

Dawson, Roger. *Secrets of Power Negotiating: Inside Secrets from a Master Negotiator*. 15th anniversary ed. Pompton Plains, NJ: Career Press, 2012.

Diamond, Stuart. *Getting More: How You Can Negotiate and Succeed in Work and Life*. New York, NY: Three Rivers Press, 2012.

Dvorak, Petula. "Antoinette Tuff's 911 Call on Ga. Shooting Suspect Is a Portrait of Poise, Compassion," *Washington Post*, August 22, 2013. Retrieved October 21, 2013 (http://articles.washingtonpost.com/2013-08-22/local/41435570 _1_assault-rifle-sandy-hook-elementary-school-911-call).

Fisher, Roger, William Ury, and Bruce Patton. *Getting to Yes: Negotiating Agreement Without Giving In*. New York, NY: Penguin, 2013.

Gladwell, Malcolm. *Outliers: The Story of Success*. New York, NY: Little Brown, 2011.

Hagen, Shelley. *The Everything Body Language Book*. 2nd ed. Avon, MA: F + W Media, 2011.

Huffington Post. "James Franco Talks Gay Rumors, Reveals Instances of High School Bullying (video)." January 24, 2013. Retrieved October 8, 2013 (http://www .huffingtonpost.com/2013/01/23/james-franco-gay-bullied-hollywood-star-high-school-rumors_n_2534709.html).

Kahnweiler, Jennifer B. *Quiet Influence, The Introvert's Guide to Making a Difference*. San Francisco, CA: Berrett-Koehler Publishers, 2013.

Karlinsky, Neal. "Oregon Teen Alerted Authorities in Alleged School Bomb Plot; Good Morning America." KATU-TV, May 29, 2013. Retrieved October 3, 2013 (http://abcnews. go.com/US/oregon-teen-alerted-authorities-alleged-school-bomb-plot/story?id=19277136).

Kids Right to Know. Retrieved October 2013 (https://www .facebook.com/KidsRightToKnow).

Kilbourne, Jean, and Mary Pipher. *Can't Buy My Love: How Advertising Changes the Way We Think and Feel*. New York, NY: Free Press, 2000.

Knowles, David. "Video: 14-Year-Old Anti-GMO Activist Rachel Parent Takes on Condescending TV Host Kevin O'Leary, Interview Goes Viral." *New York Daily News.* Retrieved October 14, 2013 (http://www.nydailynews.com/news/world/video-rachel-parent-takes-kevin-o-leary-gmo-foods -article-1.1420366#ixzz2kU7pfEsW).

Leman, Talia. *A Random Book About the Power of Anyone.* New York, NY: Simon & Schuster, 2012.

MADD. "Problem Solving & Negotiation Skills." Strengthening Families Program, Lesson 5. Retrieved October 10, 2013 (http://support.madd.org/docs/Lesson_5_Handout_ MADD_SFP.pdf).

Mnookin, Robert. *Bargaining with the Devil: When to Negotiate, When to Fight.* New York, NY: Simon & Schuster, 2011.

Patterson, Kerry, et al. *Crucial Conversations: Tools for Talking When Stakes Are High.* 2nd ed. New York, NY: McGraw-Hill, 2012.

Seuss, Dr. *Green Eggs and Ham.* New York, NY: Random House, 1960.

Shakeshaft, Jordan. "6 Breathing Exercises to Relax in 10 Minutes or Less." *Time,* October 8, 2012. Retrieved October 4, 2013 (http://healthland.time.com/2012/10/08/6-breathing -exercises-to-relax-in-10-minutes-or-less).

Shell, Richard G. *Bargaining for Advantage: Negotiation Strategies for Reasonable People.* New York, NY: Penguin Books, 2006.

Sills, Judith. "The Power of No." *Psychology Today,* November 5, 2013. Retrieved November 6, 2013 (http://www.psychology today.com/articles/201310/the-power-no).

Smith, Lydia. "Prison Break Actor Wentworth Miller Opens Up About Suicide Attempts Over Sexuality." *The Mirror.* Retrieved November 2, 2013 (http://www.mirror.co.uk /3am/celebrity-news/wentworth-miller-opens-up- suicide-2790357).

Stone, Douglas, Bruce Patton, and Sheila Heen. *Difficult Conversations: How to Discuss What Matters Most.* 10th anniversary ed. New York, NY: Penguin Books, 2010.

Tartakovsky, Margarita. "6 Strategies to Become a Better Communicator." *Psych Central.* Retrieved January 22, 2014 (http://psychcentral.com/blog/archives/2013/10/22/6 -strategies-to-become-a-better-communicator).

Tartakovsky, Margarita. "Therapists Spill: How I Set & Sustain Boundaries." *Psych Central.* Retrieved January 22, 2014 (http://psychcentral.com/lib/therapists-spill-how-i-set -sustain-boundaries/00017954).

University of Massachusetts. "The Wind and the Sun." Aesop's Fables. Retrieved November 1, 2013 (http://www.umass .edu/aesop/fable.php?n=31).

INDEX

ABOUT THE AUTHOR

Alexandra Hanson-Harding has written more than twenty books for kids and adults. She has written about everything from ancient Rome to modern physics. Science has long been one of her favorite subjects to write about. She has also written more than one hundred articles, mostly for young people, on a wide range of subjects. In addition to writing, she also likes to draw and paint, read all kinds of books, and spend time with her family—sons Moses and Jacob and husband Brian—at their home in New Jersey.

PHOTO CREDITS

Cover Pressmaster/Shutterstock.com; p. 5 Theo Wargo/WireImage/Getty Images; p. 7 JumpStock/iStock/Thinkstock; p. 8 Purestock/Thinkstock; p. 11 Kevin Lamarque/Reuters/Landov; p. 14 Featureflash/Shutterstock.com; p. 15 © iStockphoto.com/Michael Krinke; p. 18 Mike Cherim/iStock/Thinkstock; p. 20 ChinaFotoPress/Getty Images; p. 22 Monkey Business Images/Shutterstock.com; p. 23 Bill McCay/WireImage/Getty Images; p. 25 knape/Vetta/Getty Images; pp. 28–29 Charles Knox/Shutterstock.com; p. 31 Fuse/Thinkstock; p. 32 Ivy Close Images/Landov; p. 37 auleena/Shutterstock.com; pp. 38–39 Creatista/iStock/Thinkstock; pp. 40–41 ColorBlind Images/Blend Images/Thinkstock; p. 44 Arena Creative/Shutterstock; p. 48 Eddie Brady/Lonely Planet Images/Getty Images; p. 50 cristovao/Shutterstock.com; p. 52 Helder Almeida/Shutterstock.com; cover and interior graphic elements Artens/Shutterstock.com (figures, urban environment), LeksusTuss/Shutterstock.com (abstract patterns)

Designer: Michael Moy; Editor: Heather Moore Niver; Photo Researcher: Cindy Reiman